A New True Book

FIRE FIGHTERS

By Ray Broekel

This "true book" was prepared
under the direction of
Illa Podendorf,
formerly with the Laboratory School.
University of Chicago

 CHILDRENS PRESS, CHICAGO

*The author thanks
Chief Skip Emerson,
Ipswich Fire Department,
for his help.*

PHOTO CREDITS

Harvey Eisner — 2, 4, 8, 9, 10, 11 (bottom right), 12 (top and bottom) 13, 14, 16 (left), 18, 20, 21 (top and bottom), 22 (top), 26 (top and bottom), 30, 32 (top), 34, 35, 37 (top), 41 (top and bottom), 42 (top and bottom).

Chicago Fire Department — 7 (top and bottom), 11 (bottom left), 22 (bottom), 25 (top and bottom), 28 (top and bottom), 32 (bottom), 37 (bottom), 38 (all 3 photos).

Christopher J. Naum — 11 (top), 16 (right), 24, 44.

Cover: Harvey Eisner

Library of Congress Cataloging in Publication Data

Broekel, Ray.
    Fire fighters.

    (A New true book)
    For grades 1-3.
    Summary: Briefly discusses the work, uniform, and tools of fire fighters and describes a variety of fire trucks.
    1. Fire fighters — Juvenile literature.
[1. Fire fighters. 2. Fire engines]
I. Title.
TH9148.B76   628.9'25   81-7655
ISBN 0-516-01620-2   AACR2

TABLE OF CONTENTS

4

FIRE! FIRE!

Listen to the sirens.
Whoo! Whoo! Whoo!
Listen to the bells.
Clang! Clang! Clang!
The fire trucks are
rolling. Fire fighters are on
them. Soon the fire fighters
will be at the fire. They
will put out the fire.

FIRE FIGHTERS

Who can become a
fire fighter?
A woman? Sure.
A man? Sure.
To become a fire fighter,
a person must pass a test.

Part of the test is to know the answers to questions.

What are some of the questions about?

- How to fight fires
- How to prevent fires

What else must a person
do to pass the test?
- Be strong and healthy
- Be able to work hard

What are a few things a
fire fighter does?

- Drives fire trucks
- Climbs ladders
- Uses fire hoses
- Saves people

12

SPECIAL CLOTHES

What does a fire fighter wear?

- boots
- a helmet
- a kind of coat

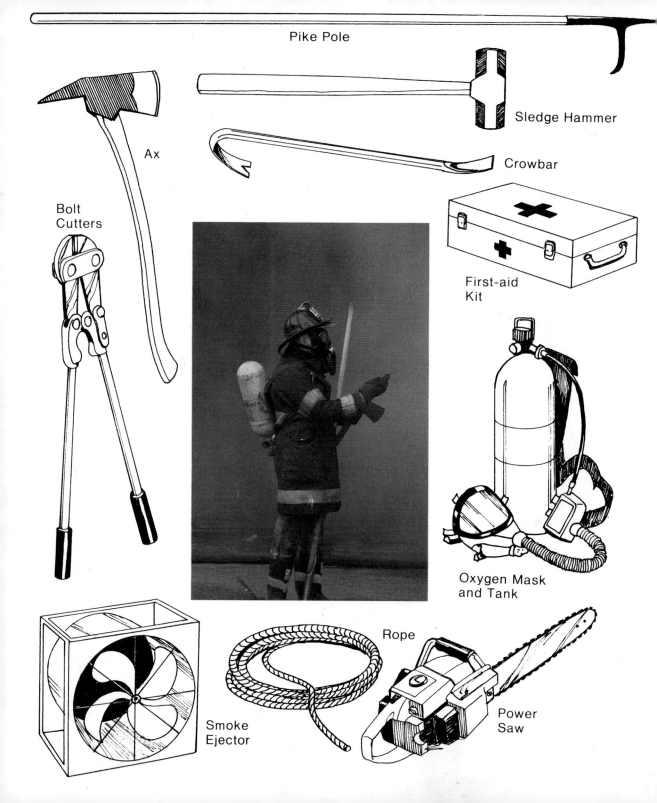

Pike Pole

Ax

Sledge Hammer

Crowbar

Bolt
Cutters

First-aid
Kit

Oxygen Mask
and Tank

Smoke
Ejector

Rope

Power
Saw

SOME FIRE FIGHTER TOOLS

What are some of the
tools a fire fighter uses?

- an ax
- an extinguisher for putting out small fires
- a nozzle
- first-aid kit
- a hose
- a wrench
- oxygen

THE HOSE

The hose is fastened to a fire hydrant.

The fire fighter then uses a wrench. The wrench opens the hydrant. Now water flows in the hose.

18

LADDERS

Fire fighters use ladders in different ways.

Suppose people are inside a burning building.

The people can be saved. They can go down the ladders.

Fire fighters also go into buildings from ladders.

Then they fight the fire on the inside.

THE FIRE TRUCKS

Some fire trucks are also
called fire engines.
Most trucks and engines
are painted red.

But they come in other colors, too.

What colors are the fire trucks where you live?

Hook and ladder truck

Pumper engine

A pumper engine goes out on all fires. This engine pumps water from a hydrant. Then the water flows faster through the hoses.

A straight-ladder truck may go to a fire.

The fire chief uses a special car.

The chief uses the siren when going to a fire.

At the fire the chief tells the other fire fighters what to do.

These big trucks are
aerial ladder trucks. Their
ladders can reach high
places.

This hook and ladder truck
is old. It has
two drivers. See
the driver in the back.

Some hook and ladder trucks have one driver.

But one kind has two drivers.

One of the drivers sits in back.

That driver steers the rear wheels.

FIREBOATS

Fire fighters work on the water, too. Some cities have fireboats.

The fireboats help fight fires on the waterfront.

AT A FIRE

What is the first thing fire fighters do at a fire?

The fire fighters must get people out of burning buildings.

The safety of those people is most important.

Then the fire fighters use
the hoses.

Sometimes fire fighters
water down nearby
buildings. That helps keep
the fire from spreading.

The people are safe.
The fire isn't spreading.
Now the fire fighters go
to work. They put the fire
out.

Fire fighters fight fires.
What else do they do?
Sometimes there is an
accident.

Fire fighters help save the
people who are in the
accident.

Some fire fighters visit schools.

They visit stores and factories.

They check the buildings.

They make sure the buildings are safe for people to be in.

Some towns don't have a regular fire department.

These towns use volunteers.

When a fire starts they are called.

They leave their jobs.

They leave their homes to fight the fire.

All fire fighters help people.

We need fire fighters.

They are our friends.

WORDS YOU SHOULD KNOW

accident(AK • sih • dent) — an unexpected happening

aerial ladder(AIR • ee • uhl LAD • der) — a ladder on a truck that goes up very high

ax(AKS) — a hand tool used to chop or cut

extinguisher(ex • TING • wish • er) — something used to put out fires

flood(FLUHD) — to fill with water; overflow

flow- to move in a stream

foam- a mixture of tiny bubbles used to put out fires

healthy(HEL • thee) — to be in good condition; normal

helmet(HEL • mit) — head covering made of a hard material; hard hat

hydrant(HY • drant) — an outlet from a water pipe

nozzle(NAHZ • uhl) — a metal spout at the end of a hose or pipe

oxygen(OKS • ih • juhn) — a gas which is needed for life

prevent(pree • VENT) — to keep from happening

pump- a thing used to pull water from one place to another

pumper(PUMP • er) — a machine which moves water

siren(SY • ren) — something used to make a loud warning sound

test- to find out if a person knows about a subject; to question

volunteer(vahl • un • TEER) — a person who does a job without pay

wrench(RENCH) — a tool used for holding and turning nuts and bolts

Dear Reader:

You can help fire fighters prevent fire. Never play with matches, lighters, stoves, fireplaces, or barbecues. Fire can hurt you.

If a fire happens go outside. Get someone to help you call the fire fighters.

INDEX

About the Author

Ray Broekel is a full-time freelance writer who lives with his wife, Peg, and a dog, Fergus, in Ipswich, Massachusetts. He has had twenty years of experience as a children's book editor and newspaper supervisor, and has taught many subjects in kindergarten through college levels. Dr. Broekel has had over 1,000 stories and articles published, and over 100 books. His first book was published in 1956 by Childrens Press.